# OPERA ON TV

## james lowell brunton

the operating system print//document

OPERA ON TV

ISBN: 978-1-946031-52-5
Library of Congress Control Number: 2019943441

copyright © 2019 by James Lowell Brunton
edited and designed by ELÆ [Lynne DeSilva-Johnson]

is released under a Creative Commons CC-BY-NC-ND (Attribution, Non Commercial, No Derivatives) License: its reproduction is encouraged for those who otherwise could not afford its purchase in the case of academic, personal, and other creative usage from which no profit will accrue.

Complete rules and restrictions are available at:
http://creativecommons.org/licenses/by-nc-nd/3.0/

For additional questions regarding reproduction, quotation, or to request a pdf for review contact operator@theoperatingsystem.org

*This text was set in 20 db, Freight Neo, Minion Pro and OCR-A Standard.*

Cover uses art from Juan Kasari's "It was meant to be a perfect society" series, (2008-10) with permission; more at http://www.juankasari.com/meant.pdf

*Books from The Operating System are distributed to the trade via Ingram, with additional production by Spencer Printing, in Honesdale, PA, in the USA.*

the operating system
www.theoperatingsystem.org
operator@theoperatingsystem.org

# OPERA ON TV

*for Emily*

# [CONTENTS]

## ONE

SENTENCES ON DIDACTIC ART — 11
WHAT ART IS LEFT — 13
Q&A WITH THE ARTIST — 14
AFTER THE WORDS — 15
LECTURE 1: SOCIAL ANTAGONISMS — 16
NONCOMITTAL — 17
OPERA ON TV — 18
ON RUIN — 19
TRANSCRIPT: FEELINGS — 20
ARS POETICA — 24
LECTURE 2: THE USE OF LITERATURE — 25

## TWO

MORNING — 29
CHASE — 30
CERTITUDE — 31
ATMOSPHERE — 32
HEAT — 33
AFFECTION — 34
TRANSPLANT — 35
VISUALS — 36
STARS — 37
WINDOWS — 38

## THREE

ANYTHING VIEWED AT A PARTICULAR ANGLE — 41
AN EXERCISE IN GOOD TASTE — 42
AN EXERCISE IN DESIGN — 43
THE MUTE SWAN — 44
A LOON CALLS OUT, ANOTHER ANSWERS — 45

TALL GRASS WAVING —46
EGG — 47
AN EXERCISE IN POWER —48
POSTSCRIPT — 49
DEVICES — 50

## FOUR

LOVE POEM 1 — 53
IOWA — 54
POEM BEGINNING WITH A LINE FROM LORCA — 55
YOU ARE A FLASH IN THIS YOUNG NIGHT — 56
LOVE POEM 2 — 57
I WANT TO BUY YOU ROSES — 58
THE EMPIRE'S LONGEVITY — 59
EXPERIENCE — 60
THE ORDER OF THINGS — 61
ONTOLOGY — 62
LET DOGS BARK VICIOUSLY FROM BEHIND FENCES — 63
LOVE POEM 3 — 64

---

ACKNOWLEDGEMENTS — 67
ABOUT THE AUTHOR — 68
THE SENSORIUM SHIFT OF IMMERSION — 69

#  ONE

ONE

## SENTENCES ON DIDACTIC ART
*after Sol LeWitt*

1. Some art tells us there is always more.
2. Some art tells us this isn't enough.
3. The kind of art that wants us to do something about either condition is called didactic.
4. Usually, didacticism is off-putting and lacks musicality and/or brilliant colors.
5. If your teacher was beautiful, you will feel nostalgia whenever you are presented with didactic art.
6. It will make you smile, wryly, to yourself.
7. Nostalgia should not be dismissed.
8. I have sat alone for hours in a dark room in front of a screen for the sake of nostalgia.
9. It produces a pleasant feeling.
10. Have you ever felt nostalgic for a time period/country you have never visited?
11. Things get mixed up.
12. I was falling in love in the early 2000s watching movies made in the '80s about colonial Africa.
13. Did you mean it when you said this isn't enough?
14. Did you mean it when you said there is always more?
15. Each stage of life should be more fulfilling than that which preceded it.
16. You should at least be wiser for having survived.
17. This is becoming seductive, I can tell.
18. Did you mean it when you said there is always more?
19. Some art tells us there is always more, that this isn't enough.
20. This is the kind of art that wants us to do something.
21. When we're not sure what to do next, we look to our past for examples.
22. According to Bergson, we remember that which has use value.
23. I get stuck untangling the meaning of utility and come back to music and brilliant colors.
24. There is an undeniable link between nostalgia and nationalism, between nostalgia and the oppressive practices of past regimes.
25. A symbol is emptied of its meaning and social function and is appreciated for the attractiveness of its shape and color.

26. If the memory of pain no longer has use value, we are seduced into forgetting.
27. I remember being threatened and taken away, but most of the details are a mystery (the words, for instance).
28. What do you remember about falling in love?
29. In the fall of '01, I stopped reading newspapers, got a bad grade in semiotics, and tasted wine for the first time.
30. Some art would be more direct than I am comfortable with.
31. If an idea is beautiful, it will express itself.
32. It has been argued that fragmented art forms are privileged in the West.
33. It is tempting to offer more out of which a confessional narrative might be constructed, but you can see what kind of person I have been already.
34. This is the kind of art that wants to be enough.
35. If you had a beautiful teacher, the ideas will express themselves to you when you are alone at a much later date.

## WHAT ART IS LEFT

Here is a hungry animal afield
Here is my love with thorns in her hair

And from this music What is an enemy
but that which does not sing Perhaps

there is no silence even where
we hold our breath in the dark of our

American cars our woods our drab
fluorescence What art is left but these

devotions none beyond reproach

## Q & A WITH THE ARTIST

What does it mean to love the light more than the message? What does it mean in another medium? What does it mean to do justice to the subject? What does it mean to be the subject? What does it mean to fill the canvas with dots? What does it mean to objectify? What does it mean to ironically appropriate the gestures of objectification? What does it mean to take up space? What does it mean to evaluate on merit? What does it mean to stop working? What does it mean to repeat? What does it mean to announce your silence? What does it mean to get out of the way? What does it mean to change? What does it mean in the context of your suffering? What does it mean in the context of my suffering? What does it mean in the voice of a character from a Greek myth? What does it mean to wail into the microphone? What does it mean to adore yourself? What does it mean to be accessible? What does it mean to be wallpaper? What does it mean to reproduce? What does it mean now that twenty years have passed? What does it mean if I add a comma here? What does it mean if we skip this one? What does it mean if you feel proud of it? What does it mean if we tell our parents? What does it mean if no one reads it? What does it mean if I must hide it under the bed? What does it mean if the syntax feels familiar? What does it mean if everything feels familiar? What does it mean if this makes you angry? What does it mean to win a prize for it? What does it mean to buy it for its color? What does it mean if there are birds in it? What does it mean if we reference Freud? What does it mean if we reference Foucault? What does it mean if I made this in my pajamas? What does it mean if it makes you laugh? What does it mean to be in print? What does it mean to read it aloud? What does it mean without line breaks? What does it mean to strike a posture of coolness? What does it mean to be earnest? What does it mean to be oppressed? What does it mean to speak from this place? From this one? What does it mean to your movement? What does it mean to your subjectivity? To mine? What does it mean if it describes a dream? What does it mean to speak for you? What does it mean to reorder the sentences? What does it mean if we teach it? What does it mean to the department? What does it mean if you get paid for it? What does it mean if you don't? What does it mean in the long term? What does it mean to the state? What does it mean in another language? What does it mean in this one? In this one?

## AFTER THE WORDS
*after Juan Kasari's photograph "Perfect Model for the Society, 1"*

I used to pretend
It was more than beauty

I was after the words
Now ask where

Are the yellows & blues taste
Of night where graffiti

Floodlights
Concrete & chain link

I breathe now
The crackling air

## LECTURE 1: SOCIAL ANTAGONISMS

I feel out of words but the others have so many:
*Two antagonistic identities cannot be expressed*
*on the same representational plane.*

Outside the lecture hall is a sculpture garden
where a middle school boy asks his teacher:
*Is there any*
*naked men in here?*

She says:
*There is one* and there is
an audible sigh.

## NONCOMMITTAL

Warhol worked with the same rock 'n' roll and opera records blaring over and over again in an attempt to make room for "instinct," to "remove all the hand gesture from art and become noncommittal, anonymous." Strange overlap of industry and nature, both being anonymous in their ways. If subject is an invention of language that we have stepped into, surely we may step out again, as into a natural state. What an assumption. There are so many ways of keeping busy, and this is another one. ("It gives me something to do.") There are surely worse ways to spend one's time. How to break from the language of negation and denial. Perhaps a posture of indifference. ("But I didn't need it then like I would later on.") Perhaps by untying oneself and becoming, thereby, an untouchable object in a mess of brightly colored distractions. How else to escape all these plots, all these sentences. ("If I'd gone ahead and died...")

OPERA ON TV

"We can't experience it
the way they did
a century ago." Still,
when the lights go down,
quiet; when the tidal wave
comes, running; when
the firing stops, pain,
the taming of pain
into art, memory,
or forgetting. This theater
is electric; I will go home
with the person I want. Still,
when it ends
we are happy to take
the electric streets, leaving
someone else's nightmare
behind us.

## ON RUIN

A woman is said to be ruined
by certain acts committed by her
or visited upon her by force or choice.
Food left out can go to ruin,
as can talents uncultivated.
A man is said to be ruined by drink or by woman.
Anything that was to be used for one purpose
and is used for a different one or not at all
may be called a ruined thing.
What is left after use may be called ruins.
Ruins are said to be beautiful.
They inspire awe and pity, sometimes nostalgia,
given their relationship to time.
Ruins are visited, looked upon, and photographed.
They are valued for the strange ways
they break up the light.

— Let's turn it on its side.

## TRANSCRIPT: FEELINGS

— You think we'll be able to hear it better that way?
— That's what I want to see.
[pause]
— I don't know if I like it this way.
— Why not?
— I just don't think it speaks to me in the same way it did before. It feels like a command; I don't know I want to relate to it in this way.
— You're letting your trust issues interfere again.
— Excuse me?
— Look, wait, I'm not saying your feelings aren't valid, I'm just saying maybe they don't have any relevance to this particular project.
—So you basically just invalidated my feelings.
— [silence]
— Well?
— Look, I think we just need to put our feelings aside on this one and just position the thing in the way that makes the most sense.
— Our feelings or my feelings?
— Look, I didn't even bring my feelings up at all.
— And that's as it should be?
— Yeah, maybe.
— This is frustrating.
— It doesn't help that it's so heavy. Or that I forgot my gloves.
— Stop changing the subject.
— Look, I'm not. I just, I just really want to have done with this part of it and move on, don't you?
— Yes, actually.
— Great. Well, then let's have a look at it from the other side. Can you reposition the light, please?
— Sure.
— Good. Now see how it glints here and how the shadow now falls on the smoothest part?
— Sure.
— I like what that says about vulnerability, don't you?
— I don't know. What is it saying?
— Something about hiding what's actually most desirable, most serene, perhaps what's wholly untouched.

— But if we're hiding it, aren't we just reinforcing the illusion?
— Well, not if we make it interactive.
— How so?
— Well, people could move the light around. Like this. [creaking noise]
— It makes a lot of racket, that.
— Yeah... Well, we could oil it I suppose.
— Sure. But how will people know they can touch it?
— Uh. Hm. I guess we could hang a sign on it, couldn't we?
— That seems like a lot of work. Is this part of it or a set of instructions?
— It could be both.
— I don't like the ambiguity. Feels a little too easy to me, a bit clichéd perhaps.
— No, no, I get you. What if the sign were something really punchy so that it really seemed part of the work?
— Like what would it say?
— "Touch me"?
— "Touch me"?
— "Touch me."
— Like in all caps.
— Yeah. Stenciled font, maybe.
— [sighs]
— Yeah.
— Does that apply to the rest of it?
— What?
— I mean are we instructing them to touch everything or just the light?
— Oh, wow, just the light, of course.
— Right.
— You don't like it.
— No, it's not that. Really, I think they should be touching the light as they see fit. Just, how are we going to convey that the light is fair game but it's hands off the rest?
— Maybe we're going about this wrong. Maybe we should consider letting them touch it.
— But it would get all smudged.
— Just on the smooth side.
— Yes, but still. All those fingerprints.
— Maybe that could be part of it, too.
— Now, see, we're back to this lack of intention thing that I find really problematic. This isn't, like, some performance where people just do stuff and we comment on it, right? We put this here for a reason.

— Did we?
— I sort of think we did. We must have.
— But are we fully aware of the driving forces behind our actions? And, isn't this giving up of control a way at pushing against the invisible structure that brought us to this predetermined point in the first place?
— Well, now you're talking about free will.
— [loudly] Right.
— Well, I think that might be beyond the scope of this project.
— Yeah, you might be right.
— I mean, I am sort of into the idea of letting them touch it, I guess. Mostly it's the smudges, really. It's like, their indexical traces are not part of the project, you know?
— I know, I know. What if we cleaned it? You know, what if we just kept some window cleaner and a rag nearby?
— Like where they can see it?
— No, no, I think that would confuse things more. We could have someone come by each night and wipe it down, though.
— Sure, sure.
— So do we agree that this side should be on the ground?
— I didn't say that.
[sound of vehicle passing, radio]
— So what are you saying?
— Isn't the side on the ground now, doesn't it have that part that sort of sticks out?
— Yes. See, that's why it's off kilter. It's tilted some because of that sticking out part.
— I like the sticking out part. It suggests to me an object reaching out of itself, there's a struggle against impossibility.
— That feels like mapping a narrative, like this narrative of human struggle, onto this object that—
— Well, that's what I'm saying, it blurs the boundaries between object and subject in that way.
— That just feels cheap to me. Like it's been done.
— What do you mean?
— Like, come on, isn't that cliché, this narrative of human struggle business?
— Okay, forget I said that part, but the part about blurring boundaries.
— Again, I'm just not sure it's saying anything new. This isn't the '90s, right?
— No, it isn't. I'm pretty aware of what decade we're in. I'm not saying, I mean, I'm saying that that's the whole point, isn't it, of all

our endeavors, is to define boundaries and push them and, you know, to like stake out territory, stake out ground.
— Now it sounds like you're envisioning this as a political piece.
— Well, it is.
— How so?
— I mean in the sense that everything is.
— Sure, sure.
— But I can see your point, I concede the point about the sticking out part being in the dirt. I'm fine with it. Okay?
— Okay. And I really do think, I mean, I really do, that the moving around the light aspect will do that work you were talking about. I really do.
— Really?
— Yeah.
— Should we try it on side C as well just so we've covered all our bases?
— [sighs]
— What?
— No, you're right, you're right. We should be thorough.
— So?
— So I'm just tired is all. I've forgotten my gloves and my hands are really cold.
— Here, let me see them. Yes, let's go in for a moment. We'll find an extra pair someplace.
— Thanks.
— Sure. We should talk about alternate colors, too.

# ARS POETICA

This is working, but for who?
I am tempted to write *tell me*. But I know
I will receive no response, and you know
you are not obliged to anyone
without a badge or the ability
to make you feel small. I try
to give you something of more substance
but objects become awkward in my hands.
I am working in the dark. I am speaking
metaphorically. I once had a goal in mind
that involved confusing you a little
to put you off my track.
You would have otherwise found me
at the end of the line
like a small animal at the base of a tree.
But this, too, seems like a bad approach,
and so I have tried to leave it.
What I have saved is a tendency to rest
on certain images—streets at night, stars
visible in the Western hemisphere
in the summer months. I cannot,
and shall no longer try,
to predict your sympathies.
I cannot pretend to love you.

## LECTURE 2: THE USE OF LITERATURE

The man at the lectern sighs, runs his hands through his wild hair and says "this is very sort of a weak kind of a thing, as opposed to what is on the handout I've given you." Directing the audience to the handout, he continues, "you can read it or not," then proceeds to read it to us. I mull over the proposition that all words are things and that things are words, yes, but also something else. Meanwhile, the man at the lectern shows a film. He says "in this film, well, I'll just show you the clip, which will sort of express what happens." What happens is the placement of a severed female head onto a plate. The six females in the audience are as quiet as six severed heads on as many plates.

I begin to grow dimly aware of myself and my limitations. The man at the lectern says "in the search for meaning, there is a horizon of unreachable wholeness." I begin to feel like a vanishing horizon. I visualize a vanishing horizon, a corona, an aura, a halo. I think of the moon, of skin drained of its blood, of clusters of stars on a cold night in December in a gun metal sky. I begin tasting the words that make me a thing. They taste like salt.

The man at the lectern declares: "It is only a thing if you use it for something." A woman in the third row nods in agreement or perhaps to assure him she is listening. She looks very tired and I wonder if she will go back upstairs to her office or go home after this, and what she will do at home, if there is a child to put to bed or a cat or a grown up person to feed, and if she will listen to music after the work is done, and what kind. I snap back to attention. I wonder at the tools at my disposal, at the possibility of transcendence or beauty in such a place. I chew on that word—*beauty*—until I imagine the taste of sugar, until I hear applause, feel the lights go on, hear someone ask "Are there no questions?"

TWO

MORNING

In some instances, there are doves by the water producing foreign music in the early light. In others, a memory of doves. There is a certitude in the shock of waking; whatever else is uncertain, at least there is this: you have emerged into a difficult consciousness again. What clarity there is in waking. It is bodily. You are new skin hitting the morning air, abundant with facts.

# CHASE

There is pain in the middle of a day. In shades drawn down against the daylight, in watching the house cats sleep in the long stretches when you're usually out and then watching them grow wilder as the shadows lengthen toward suppertime. When they dream we always guess they're chasing something that could be caught. Their paws twitch, and their mouths, too— something always dies in their dreams. There is pain in watching anything sleep, dead to this world, as they say. There are other worlds besides, and how one feels about that depends largely on which world one inhabits, who else is there. (Does the wind blow? Is there a mist rolling in from the sea or is it just rain falling, far from any coast?) There is pain in the middle of a day, in watching anything give chase. They run farther and farther out. And the arc of their return, if it exists, is invisible. There is pain in minding the clock and the pill bottles for the one who sleeps, but really it is just the pain of boredom, the sort one feels in childhood, waiting for the next sound, the next taste, the next promise of something amazing. There is a state of expectation in the chair by the side of the bed, watching, trying to distinguish an arc in a day that, like all days, though you perhaps have not realized it until now, has no arc.

# CERTITUDE

Would that one could wrestle meaning out of every little thing, that all might serve us. Instead we are left with remainders; one can ignore or revel in them. One might even worry over them, though what good would that do. In those instances, remainders might be referred to as "details." The air was fine, for instance, and a lovely evening came on about 8:30, which seemed designed for us to walk amid for the purpose of rediscovering each other at the day's end, and then, there at our feet, was a dying infant grackle on the sidewalk—a detail one would just as soon forget, or preferably, would not have encountered at all. One must resign oneself to such details. They are what's left over after we've done all our limited powers allow, which in this case amounts to walking on, becoming tired, and walking home by a different route.

# ATMOSPHERE

What details are important? She watches the cat sleeping on his perch, his ears turning like satellites in search of some intelligible signal, some warning. Outside, sirens amid the whirr of morning traffic. So this is the world she will step into after her coffee, after the air inside becomes too stale and still and no more of it can be tolerated. There is no mystery today, no mystery and no elation. Is that what we are looking for? In what details can these be found? Certainly not in the traffic nor this endless western sky in the full light of day. What is wanted is evening, its obfuscation, its insistence that this could be any place at all, could be any other place but here. What is wanted is the place evening creates, existing nowhere and outside of time: distant invisible towers with their blinking red signals, primal attractions.

# HEAT

Makes the machinery unbearable. Makes the wind a furnace. Makes the birds seem brave. Makes inequalities more apparent. Makes the leaves ghosts in the unbearable sky. Makes reason a brave bird on the horizon. Makes the horizon a glass wall melting in the distance. Makes objects malleable. Makes people malleable. Makes these equivalencies bearable. Makes relief starker. Makes bodies more bodily. Makes the earth more concrete. Makes seductive its own terrible monotony.

# AFFECTION

Dear one, have you noticed how tired the grackles seem, what effort it takes to lift their full bellies aloft onto the humid air? All day they gorge themselves and grow heavy. We frighten the little gluttons away when we pass, when we sidestep the sprinklers, laughing. We have said things to hurt one another and still there is joy down there someplace like a vein of ore underground. One of us is always breaking something. Clumsy and careless are we. The grackles know it, and with great resignation, they scatter, they throw themselves into the trees. I notice no kind of affection among them, only sharp beaks and cold eyes; but it is possible, it is quite likely, that I have missed something.

## TRANSPLANT

Do these Midwest hours render you speechless? Is it their sameness, their gradual changes, and then the terrible suddenness all of it must yield—a storm with no warning, a wreck in the field? This is the time of life for it, midway through. It is summer. There is the grinding away of work, the need to produce even on days labeled free. Let's go to a coast, we think, imagining that this middle is to blame. Dry heat, hot wind, empty landscape. Its middling ways are tiresome. Do as we must, must as we do. On hot days and cold, runners and cyclists up and down the street, crashes in the intersection, bass thumping or thunder sounding from the next county over. Sometimes there is nothing here and we are bored and sometimes we merely lack inner resources, as they say. Sometimes we are afraid, sometimes they are afraid. When rendered speechless do you attach slogans to your shoulder bag or car or t-shirt? Sometimes they are afraid, sometimes we are. Of the sameness, the gradual changes, the terrible suddenness we must yield to and bear alone. We sit on porches, we look out windows. We go running toward the sound of the crash.

# VISUALS

Carefully they measured. Carefully they rowed their boats onto the sea and waited, measuring at regular intervals. I sit very carefully watching the police drive up, down, and around. There and there. None of this has been put together very well, as now a cottontail rabbit runs across the street on a diagonal. Look, I haven't chosen the colors of any of these items, nor their speed, only their inclusion. The dialogue might be important—I have failed to note the two women and the boy, speaking to or at each other, three points of a triangle. None of these colors you haven't seen before, and so they are omitted. Much is omitted. At any point we may lapse into fantasy because of these omissions. Elsewhere the boats are anchored, the sonar sings. I do not care what the boy is thinking. A boat is held firm in its chosen position and its coordinates have been noted with much redundancy. This is how we prepare for the accidental. Tabulation and exactitude. This is how we tidy up, omitting the context, which is deemed un-recordable. Here, a visual aid would be helpful.

STARS

We are not stars. The star as metaphor yields brightness (itself a metaphor), burning (still), distance, a vague sense of the eternal. No need to go on. We are not stars.

## WINDOWS

We are often to be found looking out of windows. The curiosity has left our eyes. Everything, though, is new to the cat. The blue jay is a terror: screeching, dropping from the high branches like a dead man cut down from a noose, collapsing onto his prey, and up again, hopping stiffly from limb to limb like a wind-up toy. He is an uncanny being; the cat recognizes this immediately and is justifiably unsettled, having seen through the moment into another significance.

**THREE**

## ANYTHING VIEWED AT A PARTICULAR ANGLE

> gives an effect of distance and proximity,
> becomes a thing beheld,
> makes me beholden, knowing
> my debt to an object. Anything
> viewed at a particular angle (parallax, grief)
> becomes an object, becomes visible,
> capable of being touched
> even if light years out or alone
> (celestial body, your head in my hands),
> makes me aware of being an object
> capable of being touched.

## AN EXERCISE IN GOOD TASTE

One's passion should run parallel with its object, as closely as possible, into the foreseeable future, asymptotic. Do not merge with the object nor with the theory treated as object. Mind the distance formed by desire and object doing their work of leading and being led at turns. Be led. Be repelled in turn.

## AN EXERCISE IN DESIGN

Lay your hands on the machine. Lay your body on the field. The body can withstand so much ruin, as the field can. The harvester is driven by an unseen driver. The field's pattern is visible from the road. The design is not yours. You cannot smell the dust or hear the turning blades without stopping and leaning into the wind. There is a design in this. Dangerous road, ruined field, quiet machine in the rearview.

## THE MUTE SWAN

The mute swan, named for its reticence, must be provoked to sound, and so always has a listener. Its sound is engagement. This is not always true of sound. No intention in rain hitting the roof at night. Hearing this phrase, we are listeners now to an imagined sound, its intention unclear, perhaps indecipherable. It may be that we imagine control. It may be that there are powers in us that will not disclose their source, but only their sound, as the trilling screech owl discloses his presence but not his exact location. The rhythms of incantation are fed through us and we learn to listen to them, enraptured. It may be that the source of our power is unknown to us, that it discloses only its sound, its sound a learned rhythm, its rhythm a kind of breathing, our breath an incantation. The mute swan knows its provocation but what do we know. It may be that a body is required more than a mind. It may be that our provocation resides in us, and that the rain on the roof exists next to us, merely, and that the nostalgia we feel or deny is a stretch of the imagination, what we would incorporate to make the world seem to speak to us, ourselves only listening.

## A LOON CALLS OUT, ANOTHER ANSWERS

A loon calls out, another answers.
Again and again the same voice tells
how grief and its cause are one thing.
The listener at night may imagine
how one animal, seduced by full moon,
starts a chorus of lamentation,
insane and necessary
as wild things are, and how
one can call down after another's need
in this world endlessly
and never be heard,
how this is like waking up
to the sound of loons and the person
next to you turning in dark dreams,
and being filled with something
that sings to the moonlight, incurable.

## TALL GRASS WAVING

There is a problem of travel. A problem of speech, speaking, language, and music. There is a problem of experiment, fail, and plan. A problem of sight. Of seeing people who are no longer there. There is a problem of wishing and trying. Of trying more. A problem of action where none is wanted. A problem of stillness where things are getting away. Cues and direction. If there is a gun, it should go off. If these are lovers, they should part or kiss. A problem. Of editing, sending, and receiving. A problem of punctuation but not of spelling. Pronunciation, too, is a non-issue. Having solved the problem of transport, the buses round the corner. Still there is a problem of motion, which we have touched on already. If there is a problem of contact, some of them are unaware. There is a problem of contact. Bang. There is a problem of parting. Probably, this is the major one. Tall grass, for instance, waving silently while the water calls and calls. There is a problem of miracles not happening and of fate easily observed. There is a problem of wanting. Mostly, there is a problem of not knowing. Of fear. Of making no sound. There is a problem of not knowing how, and of parting. This is the major one, the one most easily observed.

# EGG

When we stay put have we been fixed or are we moving in a circular progression like seasons. The only tension here is the comfort constantly escaping. That is the only tension anywhere. A sound like wind in the chimney. This could happen any time. This happens all the time. We make it over again, tending. A cake in the oven, a list on the wall. We go toward. Lean in close. Again. Have you tended to the eggs. Will you put them in the batter. Good. Egg is a pleasing word. It can warm the house. You are a good sound.

# AN EXERCISE IN POWER

We have been going on like this for miles, through inclement weather, with damp shoes and with grumbling stomachs, and at last it dawns on you that our story lacks even an identifiable plot, to say nothing of a hero. Were there a hero, she would not swim or ride a horse or carry a weapon or speak into a microphone unless one of these things were absolutely necessary and it pleased her to do so. More likely she would climb a hill to a garden, fall asleep under an orange tree, put everyone off with her detached way of being. She will not look at you. Unless it pleases her, unless she knows you need looking after for her own sake as much as yours. What you do not know makes you terribly angry, enough to make you want to hate her or attempt to make her yours, either by force or blind worship.

There will be no such nonsense in this story. Rather, we shall continue onward, wet shoes be damned, until we reach the sea. Sand sticks to our feet in a pleasing way (take off your shoes, thank you). I find it agreeable; you may deal with it as you wish. The end is coming, and I see that you can feel it, glancing as you do nervously from your sandy feet to the water and back again. There may be brightly colored fish in this ocean or giant aquatic mammals that can be seen only from the boats far offshore. But our story ends here, on the sand.

## POSTSCRIPT

I began to identify unrest in the atmosphere. Did we all care too much? Not enough? I wondered. Everyone was purported to be a good kid. Occasionally there was a bad egg. But there was an aura in places, like heat rising from pavement or like a lens smeared with Vaseline. I didn't think there were enough bad eggs to account for all the wavy lines, which, in comic strips, anyway, indicated pain. It was common, I supposed, for the good to suffer, toting around in their goodness a good deal of empathy and responsibility. Perhaps they all had tension headaches. At the very least, they must have been quite tired. Some of them were bartenders; others, lifeguards. I wondered how intertwined one had to become in the life of another before the two lives no longer operated at odds. The lifeguard was paid to keep us from slipping permanently into the blue calm. But there were telltale ripples everywhere and mysterious bubbles rising to the surface. Something else was breathing under and around us. I feared I hadn't tipped the bartender well enough. I feared for my very life.

## DEVICES

Now, as then, other words for *heart*;
a command in every line break;
an un-secret code in the rhyme, scheming.
Does it sing? Do you sing? It pains us to sing
before a national audience arrives.
I sing to my love: moonlight scattering
across the frozen yard. Then, as now,
all those scattered things singing.

FOUR

## LOVE POEM 1

Most things are tragic at that age. There was a powerful urgency to everything. Every sky saturated our modest skin. Objects and atmosphere hummed in our presence. We went on visibly unharmed, oblivious. To recreate this feeling, I like to stand outside at night when it is cold, ignoring artificial light sources. Of course, I never stay long; I have always hated the cold. Coming in again is like being touched.

# IOWA

Romantically one wants to matter as matter the rolling hills of Iowa. Habitually we eat oats around a table. Bliss. Periodically we exist on the verge of legality. Periodically one is legal to certain effects that sever as love does. As hills matter so does one to another and possibly more. The oats the table the habit the legality of which prevents the question of more as love does. The question is habitually reduced to legality or love. Romantically it will suffice to love the table periodically. Habitually one must weigh the value of bliss which severs.

## POEM BEGINNING WITH A LINE FROM LORCA

I want my heart to go on without its golden petals
the moon without its promise
of fullness I want the light that warms
the apple in the tree
and warmth that goes on
without the body I want
suffering to die with the body
and death to come as light
interrupted by trees and the memory
of trees fallen apples
without distance or decay
and you in the night without memory of want
I want the night that is like your heart
waking to its own unfettered want
to light that breaks for it that rises
like a supplicant blessed

## YOU ARE A FLASH IN THIS YOUNG NIGHT

You are in your best way, dressed and sweating after
a shower. The dew is settling on your good shoes. You
are a flash in this young night. You have a fresh cut
from shaving and are discreetly bandaged. You
are sixteen, on your way to meet a first love, yours
or someone else's. You are on your way
to seeing in the dark, to briefly unlearning
the loneliness of the dark fields as seen from
the passenger side window of your friend's car
because you are a flash in this young night. You
are the girl caught between the hot vinyl door
and another tepid body's perfumed sweat
on the way home from a tired high school movie. And you
are the one who retreats back to the dark unnoticed
fields when this car catches up to the lovers,
two girls everyone recognizes, driving together down
the same dark road as this car, in which everyone
is a single sweating body trying to see into the dark
car ahead of you, guessing at what goes on there,
this car in which each body will go home alone, perfumed
sweat in all of their sheets and the new moon leaving all
dark, all imaginable, and you are a flash in this young night,
you, in your best way, fresh and cut.

## LOVE POEM 2

How does it happen that we see anyone? It happens without knowing the nuances that separate one word from its near relation. That this has always puzzled me, unconsciously until now, and that I have stated it here is an example of a trait in me to which you have attached value, whether you know it or not. Everyone should be so lucky.

## I WANT TO BUY YOU ROSES

I want to buy you roses.
I want to buy you roses with some money I have earned doing simple things with my hands, like playing guitar for strangers.
I want to trade my labor for roses in a fair economy.
Or better still, grow the roses myself in our own garden and pick them while you sleep.
I want to buy you roses because we need symbolic gestures.
I want to buy you roses because it is so easy straight people can do it.
I want to buy you roses with words that are chosen carefully for the concepts they represent. A red rose for the labour party, a white rose for the nonviolent resistance.
I want to buy you roses for the sound of your hands unwrapping the paper from the stems, of the water filling the vase in our kitchen.
I want to buy you roses because once I bought you hot chocolate instead of roses, before I could tell you I loved you.
I want to buy you roses because the hot chocolate burned my hands on the long walk back to the dormitory.
I want to buy you roses because we were teenagers.
I want to buy you roses and you will grab my tie and kiss me like in the movies.

# THE EMPIRE'S LONGEVITY

In the old times we watched stars waiting for one of them to fall or reveal itself to be a planet, brighter and less stable than the rest. In the old times indoor things (blankets, packaged foods) were brought outside to help us stay there. Favorites: stars, the drive-in movie. Favorites: soft men in steel-toed boots, a radio in every kitchen. In the old times most of what we touched was new. The requisite observation: all times are coterminous in some places. In the year of our birth someone lamented a dearth of inventiveness and questioned the longevity of the empire. Someone was afraid to go home. Favorites: facing the sun, seeing red through closed eyes. Favorites: gravel roads, rearview mirrors, the Doppler effect.

# EXPERIENCE

There were days when we put on our best clothes to go out. There were days of not getting dressed at all. Sick days. Weekends. Other inventions. There were whole days of watching the rain from indoors. There were Tolstoy and Marx. There was the benefit of experience. Having learned not to drink on Wednesdays; having learned to chart the flux of emotions by temperature, sunlight, caloric intake, phase of the moon, political oppression, and interaction with the state; having learned when but mostly when not to emote: thusly have we aged. Still, empathy and disappointments, wanting this or that out of nowhere, out of instinct. Still, a surprise. Returning to what is tactile, and still naming ("instinct," "surprise").

# THE ORDER OF THINGS

When the bell rings, someone will ask you where to go and what to do next. Neither of these matter very much, and yet you must answer. What do you say? Some days we don't do much. We get up so early and are gone from home for so long, shouldn't we return with a cure for something? But there are the domestic pleasures keeping us sane, locked away behind doors chosen by us from among several options. This is undeniably a privilege, this brooding over what we might have done, and yet might not have, if we'd only known, which we did not. There is no telling what will happen next, not specifically, that is. When the bell rings, you will snap to attention. When the door breaks, you will react on instinct. When the asylum was open, we might have been put to work in the fields there, learning to love someone else. What happened? I wrote: *I got up early today and was gone from you for so long.*

# ONTOLOGY

Being as endless splitting of one term to find the next.
Being as a classroom wherein I face forward with gum in my mouth.
Being as my whole self crystallized into the sharp end of a pencil.
Being as witness.
Being as *I have lost him/her* as you have.
Being as accessory to loss.
Being as the shoes I bought and changed into on the ivied steps outside the auditorium.
Being as listening for the love I thought new shoes might bring.
Being as the heart driving the concept into what we can identify as blood, beating.
Being as splitting into the next heart and splitting again.
Being as a quavering note escaping the brick-walled auditorium.
Being as the foreheads I have kissed.

## LET DOGS BARK VICIOUSLY FROM BEHIND FENCES

Let men shout from the open windows of moving cars.
Let the children in capes and princess dresses peer down the depths of the mirrored lenses of my shades.
Let the flags, American and seasonal, fly on every third house as cicadas sing a past buried beneath actual earth these seventeen years.
Let it be remembered that we were once seventeen and lately arrived, identified, and entered into the systems of knowing and intent.
Love, let the record show our titles and ownerships, our intent toward each other.
Let the past come up again, cyclically, to sing and spawn and die, leaving its husk on every third oak.
Let all the hidden books be placed upon the shelves of the libraries of our dreams.
Let the video keep rolling unto the end.
Let the men fall silent.
Let us sing into the night with the car windows down and all the prairie rushing in on us, speaking the depths of allowance we are given.
Let it be judged a success, a failure, a step in a right or wrong direction.
Let there be a word or a silence with consequence, direction, intent, a mirrored depth, a library, a sound like the gathering of husks.

## LOVE POEM 3

The wall, the light, the shadow are all taking this day quite seriously. They suggest I do the same. They suggest I put on your coat and move my chair into the rectangle of sun on our dining room floor. They advise paying more attention to the empty rooms, whose colors change as the day advances, and to the dreams of the cats asleep in the daytime. There is no past, they say, that could matter as much.

## ACKNOWLEDGMENTS

*The Cincinnati Review*: The Mute Swan *and* Chase
*Denver Quarterly*: The Empire's Longevity *and* The Order of Things
*Diagram*: What Art is Left
*Ghost Proposal*: After the Words, Lecture 2: The Use of Literature, *and* Ontology
*Harpur Palate*: Poem Beginning with a Line from Lorca
*The Journal*: Tall Grass Waving
*Mayday Magazine*: Transplant
*OmniVerse*: Experience
*Quiddity*: Iowa
*Salamander*: A Loon Calls Out, Another Answers
*SPECS journal of art and culture*: Sentences on Didactic Art *and* Q & A with the Artist
*Tupelo Quarterly*: You Are a Flash in This Young Night

## ABOUT THE AUTHOR

photo by Emily Kazyak

James Lowell Brunton's poems and experimental writing appear in *Denver Quarterly*, *Cincinnati Review*, *Hotel Amerika*, and other journals. He is the author, with Russell Evatt, of *The Future Is a Faint Song* (Dream Horse Press, 2014). James teaches critical theory and poetry in the Department of English at the University of Nebraska-Lincoln.

# THE SENSORIUM SHIFT OF IMMERSION:
## A CONVERSATION WITH JAMES LOWELL BRUNTON

*Greetings comrade! Thank you for talking to us about your process today! Can you introduce yourself, in a way that you would choose?*

James Lowell Brunton, author of *Opera on TV*, transguy, artist, teacher of critical theory and poetry.

*Why are you a poet/writer/artist/creator?*

Because I have to be. I'm not comfortable unless I'm working on or planning a creative project.

*When did you decide you were a poet/writer/artist (and/or: do you feel comfortable calling yourself a poet/writer/artist, what other titles or affiliations do you prefer/feel are more accurate)?*

I started using the word "poet" to describe my occupation around the time I started working on my poetry MFA. But lately I've come to rethink that, and I'm focused on the term "poiesis"—the act of bringing into being. I think this term more accurately describes what I feel compelled to do. And because I bring things into being via multiple mediums (words, drawings, and music), I've more recently begun to answer that "what are you" question with "artist."

*What's a "poet" (or "writer" or "artist") anyway? What do you see as your cultural and social role (in the literary / artistic / creative community and beyond)?*

To extend on my answer to the last question, I think an artist is someone who brings something – an object, sound, feeling, idea – that didn't exist before into being. For me, this is at once an isolated activity and a communal (cultural, social) one because the impetus to create comes from within and is an act of self-gratification, but I also want an audience/interlocutors for the finished product. I want other people to enjoy that product with me—to understand it, to get the same feeling from it, to ask questions of it and to take joy in those actions as I do.

*Talk about the process or instinct to move these poems (or your work in general) as independent entities into a body of work. How and why did this happen? Have you had this intention for a while? What encouraged and/or confounded this (or a book, in general) coming together? Was it a struggle? Did you envision this collection as a collection or understand your process as writing or making specifically around a theme while the poems themselves were being written / the work was being made? How or how not?*

I very rarely sit down to write poems with an idea in mind about a finished product. I know that if a group of poems make sense side by side, I'll bring them together into a collection, but this is never a guarantee. The poems that make up *Opera on TV* were written during a series a major life transitions: finishing school, moving to a new state, the loss of a close family member, having my first child, and starting a new job/graduate school. I spent a lot of time alone with a sleeping baby in a quiet apartment, and I found myself contemplating a lot of abstract ideas about space, light, and mood, how these things affect our self-perception, how we craft our personal histories, and so forth. Many of the poems became very similar formally (prose blocks) and thematically, and it made sense to see them as a series of meditations. It surprised me how, despite their abstractions, these poems told specific stories about my relationships, about coming out in a particular historical moment, and other topics that felt important to me. So, I felt I had done justice to my subjects in a way that made it feel urgent for me to get these poems out into the world for others to see.

*What formal structures or other constrictive practices (if any) do you use in the creation of your work? Have certain teachers or instructive environments, or readings/writings/work of other creative people informed the way you work/write?*

At the risk of sounding like a cliché, my writing practice is very much influenced by the work of Gertrude Stein and the idea of automatic writing. I don't think that we can directly access the unconscious by typing nonsense, but I do think that, for me, making poems is a way to clear space for new ideas, and to do that, I need to just let those ideas surface without much intention. When I sit down to write, I take my pencil or put my fingertips to the typewriter keys and just write—it could be nonsense words, it could be descriptions of what I see, hear, smell around me, it could be a to-do list, but it is rarely anything that sounds immediately like a "poem." I let those unconscious decisions, that stream of consciousness, set the stage for what might later become a poem once I find a rhythm or go back and look over the words later. I also write better, or more freely, after watching movies, because, I think, of that sensorium shift that being immersed in a film enables.

*Speaking of monikers, what does your title represent? How was it generated? Talk about the way you titled the book, and how your process of naming (individual pieces, sections, etc) influences you and/ or colors your work specifically.*

I wrote the title poem, "Opera on TV," the day after a trip to the movie theater where my wife and I had just seen a documentary about the 2011 tsunami in Japan, and we were both very disturbed by the images and the enormity of the event. There were ads at the theater for a few Met Opera live performances that were going to be streamed, and I remember the walk back to our car, and the stars and lit up signs, and how lovely everything was. I think the poem came out of that experience of witnessing something devastating and terrifying and being able to walk away—the documentary was like opera in that way, so the advertisements and the experience of the documentary sort of blended in my mind to create that title. I like the work that this title does for the book as a whole because many of the poems address this issue of witnessing versus directly experiencing and our sometimes troubling capacity for things like romanticization and nostalgia.

*What does this particular work represent to you as indicative of your method/creative practice? your history, mission, intentions, hopes or plans?*

This book represents a coming to terms with a lot of trauma I experienced around coming out as queer many years earlier, and it situates my understanding of that trauma in intellectual, historical, and political terms.

*What does this book DO (as much as what it says or contains)?*

*Opera on TV* experiments with what a poem is and can do. It blends personal narrative, queer history, and critical theory in diverse forms.

*What would be the best possible outcome for this book? What might it do in the world, and how will its presence as an object facilitate your creative role in your community and beyond? What are your hopes for this book, and for your practice?*

The best possible outcome for this book would be for it to find an audience. I want it to bring me closer to other creative, engaged people in queer and trans communities. I want it to start conversations that will energize other people to create and keep me energized to do the same.

*Let's talk a little bit about the role of poetics and creative community in social activism. I'd be curious to hear some thoughts on the challenges we face in speaking and publishing across lines of race, age, privilege, social/cultural background, and sexuality within the community, vs. the dangers of remaining and producing in isolated "silos."*

This book is very aware of having a specific audience. Queer people, people who read philosophy, people who think abstractly, people who have heard of Foucault are all perhaps more likely to "get" something out of this book. So, there is definitely an element of class privilege, in terms of access to education, that this book has to own. Several of the poems, especially in the first section, actually address some of these issues about who has access to and legitimacy within spaces such as the academy. But, of course, you don't have to have read Foucault to think critically about history and politics or to think abstractly—rather, you have to have been in a social position that forces you to feel critical of the way things are. And I think the attitude, the irony, and the humor in many of the poems are more important than, say, a reference to another text, to their overall impact. I'm also writing about queerness in ways that aren't designed to explain queerness to straight people, which I'm fine with.

## ABOUT THE ARTIST

Juan Kasari has a MFA from the Academy of Fine Arts, Time and Space Arts study programme, and is a visual artist living and working in Helsinki. His works have recently been shown at Sinne gallery in Helsinki, Photographic gallery Hippolyte and MUU Gallery in Helsinki, Photographic center Peri in Turku, as well as several group exhibitions in Finland and abroad.

The reality around us is composed of random events, probabilities and intentional events. They are all complex phenomena, whether visible or invisible. We as humans exist in a no man's land between things and meanings. New things and meanings emerge from the process of encounters and events around us. His installation works renders tangible states of isolation, transitoriness and ephemerality. The artworks are large abstract colour surfaces that avoid both the figurative idiom and narrativity. They are also in a constant state of change. The artificial and natural light, the layers of superimposed video projections and the viewer's presence all play upon the gallery space and the works, giving rise to new changeable meanings. Kasari's works are based on Mondrian's idea of pure beauty that is devoid of figurative or narrative content. The projections employ primary colours and their combinations. In his artistic work, Juan Kasari explores the internal tensions of humanity and microcosmoses. His previous major solo shows (*Gated Community* and *Real White Panthers*) were about real-life closed communities. In his more recent exhibitions, Kasari's visual vocabulary has become more abstract, yet addressing the same themes.

# a KIN(D)* TEXTS & PROJECTS publication

The Operating System has always understood itself as an explicitly *queer* project: not only insofar as that it was founded, consistently produces work by, and is staffed by primarily queer creative practitioners, but also in its commitment to *queering* the normative forms and expectation of that practice. If to queer something is to "take a look at its foundations and question them," troubling its limits, biases, and boundaries, seeking possibilities for evolution and transformation, then queering is written into the DNA of the Operating System's mission in every action and project, regardless of the orientation or gender of its maker.

However: while all the publications and projects we support encourage radical divergence and innovation, we are equally dedicated to recentering the canon through committing parts of our catalog to amplifying those most in danger of erasure. First, this took to the form of our translation and archival oriented *Glossarium: Unsilenced Texts* series, started in 2016, and in 2018 we made concrete our already active mission to work with creators challenging gender normativity with our *KIN(D)\* Texts & Projects* series. Projects and publications under the *KIN(D)\** moniker are those developed by creators who are transgender, nonbinary, genderqueer, androgynous, third gender, agender, intersex, bigender, hijra, two-spirit, and/or whose gender identity refuses a label.

Titles in this series through 2020 include:

    HOAX - Joey De Jesus
    RoseSunWater - Angel Dominguez
    Intergalactic Travels: poems from a Fugitive Alien - Alan Pelaez Lopez
    A Bony Framework for the Tangible Universe - D. Allen
    Opera on TV - James Lowell Brunton
    Hall of Waters - Berry Grass
    Transitional Object - Adrian Silbernagel
    Sharing Plastic - Blake Neme
    The Ways of the Monster - Jay Besemer
    Marys of the Sea - Joanna C. Valente
    lo que les dijo el licantropo / what the werewolf told them - Chely Lima
    Greater Grave - Jacq Greyja
    cyclorama - Davy Knittle

## WHY PRINT / DOCUMENT?

*The Operating System uses the language "print document" to differentiate from the book-object as part of our mission to distinguish the act of documentation-in-book-FORM from the act of publishing as a backwards-facing replication of the book's agentive \*role\* as it may have appeared the last several centuries of its history. Ultimately, I approach the book as TECHNOLOGY: one of a variety of printed documents (in this case, bound) that humans have invented and in turn used to archive and disseminate ideas, beliefs, stories, and other evidence of production.*

*Ownership and use of printing presses and access to (or restriction of printed materials) has long been a site of struggle, related in many ways to revolutionary activity and the fight for civil rights and free speech all over the world. While (in many countries) the contemporary quotidian landscape has indeed drastically shifted in its access to platforms for sharing information and in the widespread ability to "publish" digitally, even with extremely limited resources, the importance of publication on physical media has not diminished. In fact, this may be the most critical time in recent history for activist groups, artists, and others to insist upon learning, establishing, and encouraging personal and community documentation practices. Hear me out.*

*With The OS's print endeavors I wanted to open up a conversation about this: the ultimately radical, transgressive act of creating PRINT /DOCUMENTATION in the digital age. It's a question of the archive, and of history: who gets to tell the story, and what evidence of our life, our behaviors, our experiences are we leaving behind? We can know little to nothing about the future into which we're leaving an unprecedentedly digital document trail — but we can be assured that publications, government agencies, museums, schools, and other institutional powers that be will continue to leave BOTH a digital and print version of their production for the official record. Will we?*

*As a (rogue) anthropologist and long time academic, I can easily pull up many accounts about how lives, behaviors, experiences — how THE STORY of a time or place — was pieced together using the deep study of correspondence, notebooks, and other physical documents which are no longer the norm in many lives and practices. As we move our creative behaviors towards digital note taking, and even audio and video, what can we predict about future technology that is in any way assuring that our stories will be accurately told – or told at all? How will we leave these things for the record?*

*In these documents we say:*
WE WERE HERE, WE EXISTED, WE HAVE A DIFFERENT STORY

*- Elæ [Lynne DeSilva-Johnson], Founder/Creative Director*
THE OPERATING SYSTEM, *Brooklyn NY 2018*

# RECENT & FORTHCOMING FULL LENGTH
# OS PRINT::DOCUMENTS and PROJECTS, 2018-19

*2019*

Y - Lori Anderson Moseman
Ark Hive-Marthe Reed
I Made for You a New Machine and All it Does is Hope - Richard Lucyshyn
Illusory Borders-Heidi Reszies
A Year of Misreading the Wildcats - Orchid Tierney
Collaborative Precarity Bodyhacking Work-book and Research Guide - stormy budwig,
Elae [Lynne DeSilva-Johnson] and Cory Tamler
We Are Never The Victims - Timothy DuWhite
Of Color: Poets' Ways of Making | An Anthology of Essays on Transformative Poetics -Amanda Galvan Huynh & Luisa A. Igloria, Editors
The Suitcase Tree - Filip Marinovich
In Corpore Sano: Creative Practice and the Challenged* Body - Elae [Lynne DeSilva-Johnson] and Amanda Glassman, Editors

## KIN(D)* TEXTS AND PROJECTS

A Bony Framework for the Tangible Universe-D. Allen
Opera on TV-James Lowell Brunton
Hall of Waters-Berry Grass
Transitional Object-Adrian Silbernagel

## GLOSSARIUM: UNSILENCED TEXTS AND TRANSLATIONS

Śnienie / Dreaming - Marta Zelwan, (Poland, trans. Victoria Miluch)
Alparegho: Pareil-À-Rien / Alparegho, Like Nothing Else - Hélène Sanguinetti (France, trans. Ann Cefola)
High Tide Of The Eyes - Bijan Elahi (Farsi-English/dual-language)
trans. Rebecca Ruth Gould and Kayvan Tahmasebian
In the Drying Shed of Souls: Poetry from Cuba's Generation Zero
Katherine Hedeen and Víctor Rodríguez Núñez, translators/editors
Street Gloss - Brent Armendinger with translations for Alejandro Méndez, Mercedes Roffé, Fabián Casas, Diana Bellessi, and Néstor Perlongher (Argentina)
Operation on a Malignant Body - Sergio Loo (Mexico, trans. Will Stockton)
Are There Copper Pipes in Heaven - Katrin Ottarsdóttir (Faroe Islands, trans. Matthew Landrum)

*2018*

An Absence So Great and Spontaneous It Is Evidence of Light - Anne Gorrick
The Book of Everyday Instruction - Chloë Bass
Executive Orders Vol. II - a collaboration with the Organism for Poetic Research
One More Revolution - Andrea Mazzariello
Chlorosis - Michael Flatt and Derrick Mund
Sussuros a Mi Padre - Erick Sáenz
Abandoners - Lesley Ann Wheeler
Jazzercise is a Language - Gabriel Ojeda-Sague
Born Again - Ivy Johnson
Attendance - Rocío Carlos and Rachel McLeod Kaminer
Singing for Nothing - Wally Swist
Walking Away From Explosions in Slow Motion - Gregory Crosby
Field Guide to Autobiography - Melissa Eleftherion

## KIN(D)* TEXTS AND PROJECTS

Sharing Plastic - Blake Nemec
The Ways of the Monster - Jay Besemer

## GLOSSARIUM: UNSILENCED TEXTS AND TRANSLATIONS

The Book of Sounds - Mehdi Navid (Farsi dual language, trans. Tina Rahimi
Kawsay: The Flame of the Jungle - María Vázquez Valdez (Mexico, trans. Margaret Randall)
Return Trip / Viaje Al Regreso - Israel Dominguez; (Cuba, trans. Margaret Randall)

*for our full catalog please visit:*
https://squareup.com/store/the-operating-system/

*deeply discounted Book of the Month and Chapbook Series subscriptions
are a great way to support the OS's projects and publications!*
sign up at: http://www.theoperatingsystem.org/subscribe-join/

# DOC U MENT
/däkyəmənt/

First meant "instruction" or "evidence," whether written or not.

*noun* - a piece of written, printed, or electronic matter that provides information or evidence or that serves as an official record
*verb* - record (something) in written, photographic, or other form
*synonyms* - paper - deed - record - writing - act - instrument

[*Middle English, precept, from Old French, from Latin documentum, example, proof, from docre, to teach; see dek- in Indo-European roots.*]

### Who is responsible for the manufacture of value?

Based on what supercilious ontology have we landed in a space where we vie against other creative people in vain pursuit of the fleeting credibilities of the scarcity economy, rather than
freely collaborating and sharing openly with each other in ecstatic celebration of MAKING?

While we understand and acknowledge the economic pressures and fear-mongering that threatens to dominate and crush the creative impulse, we also believe that
**now more than ever we have the tools to relinquish agency via cooperative means,**
fueled by the fires of the Open Source Movement.

Looking out across the invisible vistas of that rhizomatic parallel country
we can begin to see our community beyond constraints, in the place where intention meets
resilient, proactive, collaborative organization.

Here is a document born of that belief, sown purely of imagination and will.
When we document we assert. We print to make real, to reify our being there.
When we do so with mindful intention to address our process, to open our work to others, to create beauty in words in space, to respect and acknowledge the strength of the page we now hold physical, a thing in our hand, we remind ourselves that, like Dorothy: *we had the power all along, my dears.*

### THE PRINT! DOCUMENT SERIES
*is a project of*
the trouble with bartleby
*in collaboration with*
the operating system